WHAT WENT WRONG?

How to Gain Mastery Over the Reality of Trauma and Heal Well

By

LAUREL TAYLOR

DISCLAIMER

This book is only intended to provide knowledge that is relevant to daily life. Every effort has been made to provide accurate, current, trustworthy and comprehensive information. In no way should you take this as medical advice; instead, you should speak with your physician.

TABLE OF CONTENTS

Introduction

Has your motivation ever been questioned? Why can't I just regulate my behavior, you could ask as an option. Others may take issue with our comments and ponder why we have a problem with that particular individual. It is simple to hold those close to us to a high standard and put the blame for our emotional issues on ourselves. We are now ready to begin asking new questions.

Instead of asking "What's wrong with you," Laurel Taylor advises asking "What has occurred to you" through understanding and regaining your body's knowledge through incredibly personal conversations.

Laurel covers a wide range of subjects in this book, such as what trauma is, how it develops, how it manifests, and practical advice for preventing trauma. It's a minor but significant shift in how we think about trauma, one that allows us to make sense of the past to make space for the future and open the door to resilience and healing using a tried-and-true method.

Chapter 1

The Reality of Trauma

The most frequently avoided, disregarded, rejected, erroneously understood, and improperly treated cause of human misery is trauma. When I use the word "trauma," I mean the frequently incapacitating symptoms that many people go through after going through situations that they consider to be life-threatening or overwhelming. In the recent past, "everyday stress" has been replaced by the word "trauma," as in "I had a terrible day at work." However, this usage is wholly erroneous. Even in challenging conditions, not all traumatic occurrences are also stressful.

Everybody's Individuality

Nobody is the same as another when it comes to trauma. Something thrilling to one person may ultimately prove fatal to another. The broad spectrum of risk reactions is influenced by several factors. These emotions are influenced by factors such as a person's genetic makeup, environment, family relationships, trauma experiences, and even their surroundings. We must be able to recognize these disparities. Just being aware that some early traumas can have a significant impact on how we manage and interact with the world may encourage support and compassion rather than harsh judgement, both for ourselves and others.

The most crucial lesson I've learned about trauma is that it's possible for people, particularly kids, to get overwhelmed by what we typically consider to be regular, everyday occurrences. The only people who up until recently met the description of trauma were "shell-shocked" combat veterans who had sustained significant harm, people who had been the victims of extreme abuse or violence, and people who had suffered major accidents and injuries. This limited perspective and reality are incompatible.

A person may suffer harm as a result of several small mistakes over time. Major catastrophes do not usually end in trauma. Auto accidents, including fender benders, are common triggers for these conditions.

Storms and earthquakes are examples of natural disasters, as are medical procedures that are frequently dangerous to lose a loved one.

A child may find it daunting when they fall off their bike. We'll talk more later on about these situations. For now, I'll just say that practically everyone has been impacted by trauma in some way, either directly or indirectly.

Long-lasting effects from traumatic events are possible. A traumatized combat veteran will undoubtedly jump in response to recent gunfire, as in the case of a car backfiring. It's also simple to make the connection when a victim of abuse begins to perspire in a crowded elevator. Even though our emotions are not as outwardly visible, many of us—if not most of us—who have gone through a succession of less dramatic situations have been overcome by them.

Trauma is fundamentally the loss of one's connection to one's self, one's body, one's family, one's friends, and the outside world. Due to its gradual onset, this link loss frequently passes unnoticed. We eventually grow accustomed to these minor alterations because they may happen gradually, and occasionally we are unable to notice them. Most people tend to avoid discussing the subtle impacts of trauma. We may only ever sense that something is wrong without fully understanding what is happening, particularly when our sense of self-worth, self-confidence, emotions of well-being, and connection to life gradually disappear.

When we steer clear of particular attitudes, people, things, places, and circumstances, our options become more and more limited. We are becoming less capable of achieving our objectives as a result of this ongoing creation of freedom.

Considering Health in the Modern Age
Many of the long-lasting impacts of trauma are thought to be incurable illnesses that can only be slowly cured with medicine or behavioral therapy, according to the mental health community. Drugs, even though they can occasionally be incredibly helpful, are insufficient in and of themselves, thus I disagree.

I now know that humans have a built-in ability to bounce back from disaster from the moment they are born. I believe that trauma is not only reversible but that the healing process itself may provide a path to a profound awakening and real spiritual development. I don't think we can figure out how to cure and stop most of the damage caused by trauma as individuals, families, groups of people, or even as nations. By doing this, we will considerably boost our chances of attaining our goals—both personal and social.

Chapter 2

Trauma's Initiators

It is advantageous to comprehend the most likely trauma-related causes as well as the potential symptoms that may have developed as a result. Whatever the reason, trauma is trauma. For this to make sense, it's important to concentrate on the notion that trauma can be caused by any experience, whether it's done so consciously or accidentally. A person's age, life experience, and even innate personality all affect how others see them. For instance, unanticipated loud noises, such as thunder, or irate adult screams, can traumatize infants and young children. But the fundamental elements of trauma are feeling threatened and being unable to deal with it. In actuality, life-threatening thunder and screams are very uncommon.

Various Trauma Types

Both immediately evident and less immediately apparent trauma causes fall into the two primary categories.

Visible causes include:
1. War is one of several clear-cut causes of trauma.
2. Whether it be emotional, physical, or sexual abuse, severely mistreating a child
3. The abuse, betrayal, or abandonment of a child.
4. Witnessing or being subjected to violence
5. Rape
6. Awful illnesses and injuries

Less visible causes include:
1. Minor motor accidents, especially those that produce whiplash (even fender benders), invasive medical and dental treatments, particularly when performed on children while restrained or drugged.
2. A traumatizing event is more likely when ether is used. Although we are aware of the

benefits and necessity of some medical treatments, such as a pelvic exam, some people may nevertheless feel threatened during these procedures.

3. Accidents involving falls and other minor injuries, particularly those involving children or the elderly (for instance, a toddler falling off a bicycle)

4. Fires, floods, storms, tornadoes, and earthquakes are examples of natural catastrophes.

5. High temperatures or unintentional poisoning cases illness

6. Young children alone while babysitting

7. Inactivity for an extended length of time, especially in young people (such as when wearing a cast or splint for scoliosis or having their feet turned in).

8. Excessive heat exposure, especially in infants and young children

9. Abrupt loud noises, particularly in infants and young children

Pay attention to your body.

Following reading the list, how did you feel? After reading about all the potential traumas, did you feel a little anxious? If this is the case, then what you're feeling is a normal reaction to being reminded of something that might have harmed you in the past. There are typically several viable responses. Your heart can start beating more quickly or your stomach might get tight. Even while you might not have noticed anything while you were reading, you might have felt a little queasy after finishing. Alternatively, it's likely that you simply remembered falling off your bike without being conscious of any physical responses.

It's crucial to realize that every feeling, including anxiety, worry, and other negative emotions, stems from the energy that was awakened or activated during the first overpowering event. Your body produces a lot of energy on an automatic basis to aid in your defense when you are threatened. It is important to understand that we use this energy to heal from trauma.

The symptoms that are left over frequently take longer to appear. Some of the earlier symptoms may have existed before them in the majority of cases. Though not predetermined, the timing and propensity of a symptom to manifest are. The people in this group are:

1. decreased level of emotion
2. excessive shyness preventing you from doing something, lack of physical vigor, or ongoing fatigue
3. psychosomatic disorders include but are not limited to, immune system illnesses, some endocrine disorders, such as hypothyroidism, and environmental sensitivity. Other examples of psychosomatic disorders include headaches, migraines, neck, and back problems.
4. ongoing discomfort
5. fibromyalgia
6. skin conditions and asthma
7. intestinal problems (spastic colon)
8. the severe premenstrual syndrome
9. the feeling of sadness and impending doom

10. feelings of separation, alienation, and loneliness (sometimes referred to as feeling like a "living dead")
11. reduction in planning capacity

Stable, or persistent, trauma-related symptoms are possible. Additionally, they could be irregular, meaning that in stressful conditions, they might come and disappear. It's also possible for them to live for many years underground before suddenly emerging. Rather than presenting alone, symptoms frequently manifest in groups. They frequently evolve into more intricate states and lose their connection to the original traumatic event.

Repeating Self-Consciously

There is one more symptom we need to look at before diving into the mechanism by which trauma affects the body and mind and causes long-term problems. The desire to repeat the actions that initially caused the problem is one of the stranger and more troubling symptoms that can develop from unresolved trauma.

Unavoidably, we are persuaded to enter situations that both overtly and subtly reflect the initial trauma. An illustration would be a dancer or prostitute who has a history of being sexually abused as a young child. We may relive the impacts of trauma through physical symptoms or a full-fledged involvement with the outer world.

Reenactments can take place in intimate settings, at work, in settings where accidents or disasters commonly happen, as well as in other contexts that seem unrelated. Furthermore, they could show up as mental disorders or physical symptoms. Oftentimes, when children have experienced a traumatic occurrence, they act it out in their play. Adults frequently experience pressure to relive their traumatic childhood experiences in their daily lives. The approach is the same regardless of the age of the person.

The Message that Symptoms Convey
No matter the kind of event that set off the trauma, any or all of these symptoms may appear. Furthermore, these signs can and will fade away

after the trauma has healed. To recover from trauma, we must learn to trust the messages our bodies are giving us. Alarms that go off inside the body are symptoms of trauma. If we can learn to hear these messages, become more aware of our bodies, and then put these signals to use, we can begin to heal our traumas. So, if you are dissatisfied after reading about these symptoms, you might be able to reframe your feelings as the start of your healing process. You might be grateful that your body is letting you know that you need to heal.

Chapter 3

Trauma Symptoms and Their Recurrence

Specifically, let's consider the various signs and symptoms that chronic trauma can and frequently does produce.

I want to emphasize how critical it is to recognize these typical traumatic indicators for what they are: traumatic symptoms. We receive signals from our bodies when they are in discomfort. These notifications are meant to act as a warning that something is wrong internally and needs our attention. If ignored, these messages eventually materialize as signs of trauma.

It's critical to remember that not everyone who displays one or more of these symptoms has gone through trauma and that not all of these symptoms are primarily caused by trauma. For instance, stomach pains from the illness may resemble signs of trauma. A distinction does exist, though.

Typically, flu symptoms subside after a few days. Trauma-related ones don't.

Symptoms such as hyper arousal, tightness, detachment, and denial, as well as helplessness, immobility, or freezing, are likely to appear right away after a distressing incident. We shall analyze each of these separately.

Hyper arousal

Physical symptoms of this could include a faster heartbeat, increased sweating, shallow breathing, panting, cold sweats, tingling, and tensed muscles. A racing mind, more frequent, repetitive thoughts, and worry are additional cognitive manifestations that may occur. These feelings and concepts will peak if we let them be observed, or, to put it another way, if we let them naturally flow. Following that, they will begin to vanish and resolve. As this occurs, we may experience trembling, shaking, vibration, waves of warmth, fullness of breath, a slower heartbeat, warmth, muscle relaxation, and an all-pervasive sensation of relief, comfort, and safety.

Constriction

Hyper arousal is first accompanied by a tightening of the body and a restriction of the senses when we respond to a circumstance that threatens our existence. To appropriately address the threat with all of our efforts, our nervous system makes sure that it can be identified. As a way to increase strength and efficiency, constriction modifies a person's breathing pattern, muscle tone, and posture. Blood arteries in the skin, extremities, and internal organs contract to increase the amount of blood available to the tensed, battle-ready muscles. The digestive system is also hindered simultaneously. Both shut-down and numbness are potential outcomes.

Refuting and avoiding

Woody Allen declared, "I'm not afraid of dying." I don't want to be there, to put it bluntly. Dissociation's intended function is perfectly encapsulated in this joke. We are guarded against rising arousal, dread, and suffering by it. Natural opium endorphins are released, "softening" the agony of severe wounds. Dissociation appears to be a person's go-to coping mechanism when they are facing trauma and are faced with circumstances that are now beyond their abilities to handle.

Dissociation frequently takes place at a lower energy level when denial takes place. The person can get disconnected from their feelings or memories of a certain meeting (or set of circumstances). When something happened, we could try to deny it ever happened or act as if it never did. For example, we might pretend as if nothing has happened when someone we love passes away, when we are hurt or abused, or when we are sexually assaulted since the feelings associated with acknowledging the event would be unpleasant. Another way to experience dissociation is as a body portion that is distant or nearly nonexistent. Continual pain, a sense of powerlessness, rigidity, and feelings of being frozen are classic signs of a detached physical part. The opposite of hyperarousal is a consuming sense of helplessness, which slows down the neurological system. Not everyone experiences the same kind of occasional helplessness that is felt in these circumstances. It gives off a sense of impending doom and complete helplessness. There is more to it than just an idea, a conviction, or a make-believe story. Reality exists.

Additional Symptoms
In addition to those we have just discussed, there may be more early symptoms that start to show concurrently with or shortly after those we have just described.

1. Being always alert, having intrusive thoughts, or experiencing flashbacks are all examples of hypervigilance.
2. Very susceptible to sound and light
3. Hyperactivity
4. More emotional sensitivity and startle
5. Worries and nightmares during the night
6. Uncontrollable mood fluctuations, such as sobbing or having frequent fits of wrath
7. Reduced ability to handle stress (stressed out easily and frequently) Shame and a bad view of oneself
8. Trouble sleeping

Some of these symptoms could perhaps appear years or even decades from now. You should be aware that this is not a diagnostic list. It acts as a manual to assist you in comprehending the behavior of trauma symptoms. You might see any of the following signs:

1. fears, phobias, and panic attacks
2. being mentally disorganized or "blank"
3. avoidant conduct (staying away from people, places, movements, activities, memories, or situations)
4. an inclination to put oneself in risky situations
5. behavior that is addictive (such as binge eating, drinking, or smoking)
6. a shift in sexual behavior patterns
7. memory loss and inability to remember
8. a lack of capacity for affection, nurturing, or forming relationships with others
9. apprehension towards death or a short life
10. self-mutilation (including severe maltreatment, self-inflicted wounds, and cutting) (Severe abuse, self-inflicted wounds, etc.)

11. the degradation of enduring beliefs (spiritual, religious, interpersonal)

Symptoms of trauma may be persistent and steady. They might also change their behavior suddenly under pressure since they could be unpredictable. Instead, they could spend years underground before emerging unexpectedly. Clustering of symptoms is more common than individual occurrence. Over time, they frequently become more intricate and disconnected from the original traumatic event.

Instability of Repeating

Before delving into the process through which trauma permeates the body and mind and results in long-term issues, there is one more symptom that we need to examine. Comparatively speaking, this one is a tad more difficult. One of the strangest and more concerning symptoms that can arise from unresolved trauma is the need to repeat the actions that initially triggered the issue. We are compelled to enter into circumstances that repeat the initial trauma in both overt and covert ways. A common example is a prostitute or dancer who was sexually abused as a child. Due to physical symptoms or a full-fledged interaction with the outside world, we could once again feel the effects of trauma.

Reenactments can take place in private settings, at work, in professions where frequent accidents or tragedies occur, as well as in other seemingly unconnected circumstances. Alternatively, they could manifest as physiological symptoms or mental illnesses. When kids experience terrible things, they frequently recreate them in their play. The impulse to revisit our painful childhood experiences as adults is constant. No of the individual's age, the strategy remains the same.

The Message that Symptoms Convey
Whatever the type of event that caused the trauma, any or all of these symptoms may manifest. When the trauma has healed, these symptoms may also go away. Learning to trust the messages that our bodies are sending us is essential if we want to recover from trauma.

Trauma's symptoms are internal alarms, which are its cause. We might start to heal our traumas if we can learn to recognize these screams, improve our body awareness, and use these messages. As a result, you might be able to think of feeling unsatisfied after reading about these symptoms as the beginning of your healing process. You could choose to be appreciative that your body is letting you know that healing is required.

Chapter 4

The Body's Reactions to Trauma

Brain science was a subject that interested me when I initially started studying trauma. I knew that the instinctual regions of the human and animal brains are very similar. Further realizations included the fact that prey animals rarely fear despite frequently being in danger from their surroundings. Instead, they appear to be able to recover from potentially fatal encounters fairly instantly and resume their normal lives.

Through watching videos of wild prey species, I discovered that most animals go through a similar physiological recovery process after experiencing a close call. This procedure was startlingly similar to the shivering, shaking, and irregular breathing I had seen. Several shamanic healing ceremonies that took place abroad allowed me to see this procedure in action.

It begins to tremor softly as the enormous beast stirs. As the trembling develops over time, the limbs begin to flail around uncontrollably in an almost convulsive shaking. When an animal stops trembling and begins to breathe properly and deeply, it can give oxygen to every cell in its body. The movie's scientist narrator says that the mobility of the bear is important because it "blows off tension" built up during the pursuit and capture.

The key sentence is as follows: When the bear retaliates, it is obvious from watching it in slow motion that the seemingly random limb gyrations are deliberate running actions. The appearance of the animal suggests that it deliberately picks up its running gaits again after being tranquilized to make its getaway. The bear then releases its "frozen energy" and yields through a sequence of natural, whole-body breaths.

As more and more evidence became available, I grew more and more persuaded that healing from trauma, whether it be called "reassociation" or "soul retrieval," as shamans do, is ultimately a biological or physical process that frequently has psychological implications. This is especially true when those who were supposed to protect us betrayed us throughout the tragedy. Additionally, I came to the conclusion that effective treatment approaches needed to be connected to the body. Techniques that prevent people from getting in touch with their bodies will inevitably be effective.

Time to assemble everything.

Fight, run, and Freeze

When a situation is deemed to be life-threatening, the body and mind go into "fight or flight" mode and mobilize enormous amounts of energy in preparation for either fighting or escape. With the same amount of strength, a small mother can move a ton of Detroit steel off of her child's legs when the child is pinned underneath a car. This level of power is supported by the release of stress hormones like cortisol and adrenaline as well as a significant increase in blood flow to the muscles.

The majority of the extra chemicals and energy that the mother accumulated to battle the threat are released during the 2,000-pound lift. He was pinned beneath the car, paralyzed with fear and anguish, and she wouldn't be able to do anything for him. After the body has used up all of its energy, the brain receives a signal saying the threat has passed and it is now acceptable to lower the levels of the stress hormone. The mother goes through the things mentioned when something similar occurs.

If the body does not receive the signal to regulate, the brain just continues to produce huge amounts of cortisol and adrenaline, which keeps the body in a high-energy, heightened state. The son is currently facing this circumstance. If he can't learn to let go of the extra energy, his body will continue to act as though it were in pain and impotent even after he has healed from his physical wounds. What prevents people from carrying on as usual when a threat has passed is the essential question. Why can't we simply release our tension as animals do in their natural state?

I'd like to welcome you to the Serengeti Plain, hidden away in the recesses of our psyches, where you will find the answer to this problem. Imagine a cheetah in a crouching position, its eyes fixed, and its muscles twitching in preparation for attacking an impala that is darting and moving swiftly. When you see the slender cheetah catching up to its prey at a pace of 70 mph, keep your emotions in check. The impala flops to the ground in front of the cheetah's waiting claws, which are ready to pounce on its prey's haunches. Nearly looking like it has given up and is waiting for the predator to murder it.

But the Impala that was already dead is still living. Though it could seem lifeless and immobile, the rapid pursuit is still quite stimulating to its neural system. Even if the animal is scarcely moving or breathing, its heart and brain are continuously beating. The same drugs that were previously mentioned and stimulated its desire to fly are still being pumped into its body and brain. Perhaps not immediately, the impala will be eaten. The mother cheetah may drag her (seemingly dead) prey under a bush before pursuing her ravenous offspring, who are safely tucked away.

After the cheetah has left, the momentarily "frozen" impala may awaken from its state of shock and tremble and quiver to release the enormous amount of energy it must have conjured to live. The impala will finish this process of readjusting by stumbling to its feet, taking a few timid steps, and then sprinting out in pursuit of the herd as if nothing strange had happened.

The "immobility response" of the Impala is just as important as "fight" and "flight" as a survival tactic. Also referred to as the "freeze" response, this risky survival tactic. Being a slow-moving and extremely defenseless mammal, the opossum's first line of defense is immobility. Any animal will utilize it if it is kept in a location from where it cannot escape.

The immobility response includes numbness as one of its main components. It won't feel any pain or even terror if the impala (or person) is "frozen" when it's murdered.

When they are hurt or maybe just overwhelmed, people usually use the frozen energy of the immobility reaction. Humans frequently find it difficult to get back to normal after being in this state, unlike the Impala. The emotions we need to experience to guide ourselves back to the present seem to have lost their intensity. To establish oneself as normal, we must face some challenges. In my opinion, the most crucial element in injury prevention is the capacity to regain equilibrium and balance after evoking the "immobility reaction".

How are creatures that live in the wild able to successfully revert to their natural state? The key to understanding the answer is to be able to recognize the type of uncontrollable trembling, shaking, and breathing I previously mentioned. The head park biologist at the Mzuzu Environmental Center in Malawi, Central Africa, Andrew Bwanali, received my report on my observations on ape behavior. He nodded eagerly before shouting, "Yes! Yes! Yes! True. We take great care to make sure that the animals have behaved exactly as you have described before we release them back into the wild. They won't survive if they haven't shaken and breathed in that way before being freed, he said, turning to face the earth. These people will pass away. Humans seldom die from trauma, but if we do not recover, the effects can dramatically shorten our life expectancy. Some have even called the condition "a living death."

So why can't we fight the immobility response as well as animals do? Why is it so difficult to unfreeze the energy?

External to Motionless

How people may break free from their rigidity is a mystery. Being forced to break free of this frozen state may be quite invigorating. Since they lack a thinking brain, animals in the wild behave in this way without giving it any consideration. Humans often become astonished by the strength of their energy and restrained hostility once they start to go past the immobility reaction and brace themselves against the severity of the sensations. This bracing interferes with the total energy release required to resume regular functioning. The neurological system stores unused energy, which creates an environment favorable for the development of PTSD symptoms.

Chapter 5

Healing the Wound of Sexual Trauma

The fact that one in four persons experienced sexual abuse during their teens astounded me. The conservative estimate is all it is. It seems to affect women far more frequently. Naturally, we have no way of knowing the exact number of adult victims. Unresolved social problems that are as devastating as sexual trauma are without a doubt.

Sexual trauma can result from events other than indirect sexual abuse as a child. The likelihood that sexual trauma could develop from non-traumatizing sexual experiences may be overlooked or unnoticed. A good example would be gynecological operations. When done harshly and carelessly, these can shock our pelvic and abdominal organs in a way that is similar to what those who have been sexually attacked experience. Even enemas and thermometers can be harmful emotionally when administered harshly to children.

Like other intrusive therapies, abortions can be and often are distressing surgeries performed on the internal and sexual organs. All or some of these "violations" may result in a loss of energy, a diminished capacity for sexual pleasure and connection, and other trauma-related symptoms.

The harmful impacts of childhood sexual abuse and trauma are now widely documented by scientific investigations. Numerous psychological, social, and/or physical issues frequently manifest as the abused child develops, reaches adulthood, and approaches adulthood.

Sexual Abuse Prevention
The two most urgent issues that society and people must address now are trauma and sexual assault. Science should explore them objectively as opposed to polarizing them with politics and sensationalism. Because sexual trauma has injured millions of people, we need scientific

research and the compassionate application of this knowledge. The cause of any sexual trauma is a violation. This breach could lead to the following outcomes:

1. our sacred area has been invaded
2. violation of one's energetic, sexual, emotional, and personal boundaries
3. we have shock-sensitive internal organs.
4. an unpleasant, filthy, or damaged sensation
5. massive, irrational feelings of guilt and regret
6. not being able to create strong, lasting relationships
7. the feeling of being hushed or stopped
8. strong loneliness, is characterized by a sense of being estranged from one's surroundings, from others in general, and oneself

Health Issues and Trauma

Internalized feelings of shame, fury, and dread are common when we suffer trauma. When we sense a threat, as we do when we are traumatized, our entire body is prepared to find the threat's origin and mount the appropriate defense. It follows that searching for the source of such threat elsewhere is fair. Any animal that senses danger will search for the threat's origin before scurrying away to safety in the other direction.

Although young animals will still flee from danger, they will do so in the direction of an adult source of safety, typically their mother. Human toddlers cling to their attachment figures when they see danger, just like young animals do. The fact that all people, regardless of age, seek the solace of others when they are uncomfortable or disturbed is an extremely significant distinction between mature animals and humans.

If the ones who are supposed to love and guard our abuse, humiliate, and rape us, then we are in a quandary with serious consequences. People's sense of identity and trust in their instincts are harmed by the paradoxical scenario this creates. Our sense of security and stability in the environment, as well as the caliber of our interpersonal interactions, are negatively impacted by childhood abuse because we carry these intensely conflicted early survival drives into adulthood.

Sexuality at its Best

Let's examine the crucial developmental phases of early childhood and adolescence. Children start to form a special connection with and attraction to their parents of the opposite sex between the ages of four and six. In their plays Oedipus Rex and Electra, the Greeks made use of this pervasive inclination to emphasize the devastating effects of an unanswered enigma. In new, blended, and same-sex homes, these levels (which naturally present variably)

Daughters frequently "fall in love" with their fathers, much like little boys do with their mothers, especially around the age of five. It is normal and healthy for growth to occur at this time. Children will "flirt" with their sibling's sex opposite parent when they are this young. This is more like developmental "practicing" than actual flirting in the mature, sexual sense. In other words, a teen's repertoire of peer flirtations is initially sparked and tried at home, which is supposed to be a secure place. The love that young girls have for their fathers will be evident at this time. I'd like to get married to you and start a family.

I love you too, baby, but Daddy's married to Mommy," or words to that effect, must be compassionately conveyed (and meant) by the father at this sensitive, impressionable age to promote healthy development. When you are older, you will have the opportunity to wed the one person who was made just for you and, if you so choose, have children.

As a result of misinterpreting this simple activity, which it is, what typically occurs is that the child's behavior may be improperly managed. The attitude of the parent may resemble that of a lover, emphasizing their "special" bond rather than supporting the child as they navigate their sexual development. When parents witness playful courtship, they could react awkwardly and inappropriately. This "courting" behavior typically leaves the young child feeling dominated and may worry the parent as well. Possibly, it is confusing. Clear generational boundaries are crucial in this situation, but they are commonly missing in adults who were sexually abused as children.

The relationship between parents and children is likely to quickly deteriorate during adolescence, the next critical stage in sexual development, if these lessons are not learned early on. A parent is suddenly faced with a child who is growing, who resembles the spouse they fell in love with years ago, but who may even be more beautiful. The unexpected desire for their teenager by the parents, if they are warmly erotic and uneasy with their sexuality, could result in incest panic syndrome.

The father is tied to his daughters in ways that make the idea of acting them out feel real and terrifying, particularly in the case of father-daughter relationships. He immediately stops feeling warm because of this worry and instead feels chilly and distant. As her sexual identity and sense of self develop, the daughter in this common circumstance feels both abandoned and rejected.

The father may have had inappropriate sexual encounters with her at various ages, which brings us to our final point. It's possible that he kissed her on the mouth indecently or touched her inappropriately. There's a chance that both the father and daughter found this appalling. Unfortunately, sometimes it even goes beyond.

So how can we deal with these unpleasant but common (though not inescapable) sexual feelings? Repressing these "unthinkable" emotions can cause a pressure buildup akin to a volcano, which the child will later subtly interpret as tension in the family connections. Which choices remain for me? The effects of suppressing this powerful energy include symptoms like addictions and health issues, as well as perversions like frigidity and impotence. If they act promiscuously, they might start.

Your Sexual Emotions: How to Manage Them
Awkwardness and tension make way for more relaxed, familiar interactions when parents let go of their anxiety about experiencing their sensations, set reasonable boundaries, and comprehend what children require to develop a healthy sexuality. Therefore, parents are free to express their love for their kids in non-romantic, non-sexual ways at every stage of growth.

Once puberty sets in, teenagers are less likely to feel incompetent in their romantic relationships, but they are more likely to be compulsively driven towards promiscuity to meet the needs for affection that a rejecting, repressed parent was unable to provide for them or to recreate a sexual boundary violation. In addition to creating a new legacy of life-affirming force, this will cease the transfer of sexual trauma down the generations.

Chapter 6

Effective Strategies for Preventing Trauma

Traumatic experiences will always occur in life; this cannot be avoided. It's practically a guarantee that a friend or family member will experience an accident or some other unfortunate scenario at some point. But there are numerous strategies to assist that person in avoiding persistent trauma. This section offers advice on how to interact with traumatized people, including tips for handling both adults and children. To evaluate the specific situations you are working with, you should always apply your best judgment. Here are some suggestions for assisting family members.

STAGE I

Adult First Aid: Immediate Intervention (At the Accident Site)

If necessary, life-saving medical procedures must be carried out first. Encourage a sense of safety. Unless the patient is in immediate danger, keep them warm, lying down, and calm. They could be tempted to get up, but you should resist the urgent desire for calm and the release of energy may be overcome by the sense of needing to act or do something. They might wish to downplay how bad things were and act as if nothing happened.

Keep the injured person nearby. Tell them you'll be there for them or that help is on the way. If at all possible, stay with the injured individual even after help arrives. Encourage the patient to fully experience all of their bodily sensations. A burst of adrenaline, numbness, trembling, and shivering are a few of them, along with feeling hot or cold. Of course, you can only do this if the accident wasn't really bad.

Be on the lookout at all times. Your words and deeds could aid in the person's liberation. Inform them that shaking is beneficial and will aid in their shock recovery. Once the shaking has subsided, they could feel relaxation and warmth in their hands and feet. They ought to breathe more easily and deeply. The first phase might easily take fifteen to twenty minutes.

Don't attempt it alone. Ask someone to help you digest the experience after it has happened if you need to.

STAGE II
After The Individual Is Transferred To A New Residence Or Hospital
Give yourself some time to reflect. As long as the injured person is experiencing an acute shock reaction, keep them calm and immobile. You should always take a day or two off work following an injury to allow your body to heal. Even if they believe their disability does not require them to stay at home, this is still important. This resistance may be a widespread coping mechanism for helplessness and a denial strategy.

If this initial stage of recovery is skipped, common injuries like whiplash will deteriorate and heal significantly more slowly. A wise precaution is to take a day or two off.

Allow your feelings to be felt without passing any judgment. The accident victim may start to experience a wide range of emotions, including rage, fear, grief, regret, and worry. moreover, physical symptoms such as shivering and tremor. Everything is still in order.

STAGE III
Accessing the Trauma and Generalizing It
This stage, which often follows Stage II, is crucial to releasing the trauma completely and releasing the trauma's energy that has been retained. It is crucial to assist people in remembering all of their experiences, not just those that were closely connected to the event.

Be mindful of your feelings. Be mindful that people may experience any of these stages when talking about their experiences, including agitation or excitement. They might start to breathe more quickly. They can start to sweat or their heart rate may increase. In this situation, steer clear of the incident and instead concentrate on the person's physical complaints, such as "I have a headache in my neck" or "I feel sick."

Permit the energy to flow. Continue to a more in-depth explanation of the event and the sensations as soon as the participants seem at ease and comfortable. They could detect a very minor trembling and shaking. Tell them that this is normal. Mention how the intensity of the activation reaction is lessening and how you are taking your time to gather and release the energy. This practice of moving one little step at a time is known as titration.

Prevention of Trauma in Children

Medical treatments have the potential to be the most harmful of all traumatic events that could result in physical symptoms and mental issues later in life. Many clinics unintentionally increase a child's fear after they already have it. "Papooses" are used to keep babies still during several common procedures. However, a child who fights to the degree that restraint is necessary is too afraid to be restrained without suffering the repercussions. Children who are frightened are not good candidates for anesthesia until they have achieved some degree of composure. An anxious child who is put under anesthesia is almost guaranteed to sustain trauma, frequently severe trauma. Anything can traumatize a child, including carelessly handled thermometers or enemas.

Medical professionals can perform the following to considerably minimize the trauma linked to medical procedures:
1. Parents should ensure they are with their children at all times and give them an audience.
2. Take action as soon as the kids have calmed down.

The issue is that not many medical personnel are knowledgeable about trauma or the potential long-term repercussions of these treatments. Even though medical staff are normally very concerned about the well-being of the children, they may need more information from you, the patient.

Helping a Traumatized Child

Remembering these items will help your child recuperate if they have gone through a terrible event:

1. Pay attention to the responses you receive. Give yourself a moment to relax and feel at ease by paying attention to your own internal physiological and emotional reactions, assuming there isn't a threat that needs to be addressed right away.

2. Pay close attention to your child's words and behaviors. By allowing your child to weep, quiver, or tremble naturally while they recover from trauma, you are affirming their physical responses.

3. Support these answers. You can accomplish this by expressing your acceptance to someone either vocally or physically. Put one hand, for instance, in the middle of your child's back, shoulder, or arm. Simply let the shaking happen

while saying something soothing such as, "That's okay," "It's okay to cry," (or be angry, etc.).

4. Be there for the child. After your child has stopped trembling, shaking, or crying, pay attention to their emotional reactions. Inform them that you will stay with them and listen to them no matter how they are feeling. Resist the need to rationalize away uncomfortable feelings of dread, despair, anger, rage, embarrassment, shame, or humiliation. Believe that by accepting your child for who they truly are, you will be helping them to get past these feelings.

5. Later, consider the incident once again. While helping your child get over symptoms brought on by a previous occurrence, you can facilitate the release of any stored leftover trauma energy by using play, tales, and drawings. Most of the time, the adult must first state their version of events before asking the child to give their version. Sometimes it's preferable to modify the young character's name. At

first, this might assist in establishing the necessary distance from the activity. You might also want to expose your child to commonplace things or situations that are still "charged" since they somehow conjure up the tense situation. The baby or toddler's car seat might be taken into the living room following a car accident, for instance. You can go gently toward it while carrying a little child or toddler in your arms. Finally, the child might be seated.

6. Be more rapid. Here, it's crucial to move slowly and keep an eye out for any reactions, such as stiffening, turning away, holding one's breath, or changes in heart rate. The same method may be used as a guide with every mild approach to the avoided or frightening interaction. Pace yourself by your child's demands to prevent releasing too much energy or emotion all at once. If the child appears to be becoming more agitated, you will know if this is taking place. By holding, rocking,

or gently calming a youngster, you can help them unwind.

7. It's enjoyable to engage in therapeutic play. If your child is experiencing any trauma-related symptoms, puppets, dolls, or tiny toy figures can help them get better. When a child's physical condition has improved after surgery, for example, a dollhouse bed with toy figurines of a child, parent, doctor, and nurse might be given to them. Pay close attention to how your child responds. Using the guidance, you've learned in this chapter, gently assist your child in being conscious of how their body is behaving and how to let go of any unpleasant emotions.

What Effects Does Trauma Have on Children?
Any strange behavior that appears soon after a stressful medical treatment or interaction, particularly one while under anesthesia, may be a sign that your child has been traumatized. The result of an unresolved reaction to a traumatic event is usually always compulsive, repetitive

behavior, such as repeatedly smashing a doll with a toy car. The incident might or might not be replayed during the activity. Additional indicators of post-traumatic stress disorder include:

unrelenting, despotic behavior that reverts to earlier stages, such as temper tantrums and violent acts motivated by irrational fury hyperactivity frequent nightmares or night terrors; tendency to be easily scared excessive aggression, shyness, retreat, or dread extreme clinginess severe bedwetting excessive hostility, timidity, or withdrawal, or a need for stomachaches, headaches, or other maladies with no recognized cause

Try bringing up the frightful event and watching your child's reaction to seeing whether the odd conduct is a traumatic reaction. If a child has experienced trauma, they may not want to be reminded of the event that caused it, or they may be thrilled or afraid and find it difficult to stop talking about it.

It's also crucial to understand that kids who outgrow odd behavior patterns could still be carrying the energy that created them. Because of the expanding nervous system's ability to regulate the increased energy, traumatic reactions may go unnoticed for years. You run the risk of triggering traumatic residue symptoms if you talk about a tense situation that led to changed behavior in the past in front of your child.

It need not be alarming when a traumatic symptom reappears. Despite their rudimentary origins, the related physiological systems react effectively to interventions that both include them and allow for natural healing to take place. Learning the advantages of a traumatic situation is very well received by children. All that is required of you is to create the circumstances for this to happen. Spending a few minutes with your child in a healthy way can assist to reduce the possibility of long-term consequences and enhance the child's capacity to cope with demands in life and more severe future occurrences.